A Child's Book
of
Lullabies

A DK PUBLISHING BOOK

First American Edition, 1997
2 4 6 8 10 9 7 5 3 1
Published in the United States by DK Publishing, Inc.,
95 Madison Avenue, New York, New York 10016
Visit us on the World Wide Web at http://www.dk.com

Published in Great Britain by Dorling Kindersley Ltd.

A catalog record for this book is available from the Library of Congress.

ISBN 0-7894-1507-0

Reproduced in Italy by G.R.B. graphica, Verona
Printed and bound by Tien Wah Press, Singapore

Music Arranger: Nick Fletcher
Music Copyist: Lesley Applebee

Jacket (front) and page 21, *Woman and Children*, 29 x 36 in (74 x 92 cm), Courtesy of the Fogg Art Museum, Harvard University Art Museums,
Gift of Dr. Ernest G. Stillman; jacket (front flap, detail) and page 23, *Maternal Kiss*, 22 x 18 in (55.8 x 46.4 cm), Philadelphia Museum of Art:
Bequest of Anne Hinchman; jacket (back) and pages 4 (bottom right) and 13, *Mother and Child*, 25 x 35 in (64.4 x 90 cm), The Roland P. Murdock
Collection, Wichita Art Museum, Wichita, KS; jacket (back flap, detail) and page 32, *Self-Portrait*, 9 x 13 in (24 x 33 cm), National Portrait
Gallery, Smithsonian Institution, Washington, DC/Art Resource, NY; pages 1 and 17, *The Bath*, 26 x 40 in (66 x 100.3 cm), Robert A. Waller
Fund © 1996, The Art Institute of Chicago; pages 2 (detail) and 31, *Mother and Child*, 23 x 28 in (58.4 x 71.1cm), Bequest of John J. Ireland
© 1996, The Art Institute of Chicago; pages 3 and 11, *The Family*, 26 x 32 in (66 x 81.2 cm), The Chrysler Museum of Art, Norfolk, VA, Gift of
Walter P. Chrysler, Jr.; pages 4 (top left, detail) and 19, *Sleepy Thomas, Sucking His Thumb*, 18 x 21 in (44.5 x 53.3 cm), Foundation E.G. Bührle
Collection, Zürich; pages 5 (left, detail) and 15, *Mother and Child*, 29 x 33 in (73.6 x 83.3 cm), Mr and Mrs Potter Palmer Collection © 1996,
The Art Institute of Chicago; pages 5 (right, detail) and 27, *Mother and Child*, 32 x 40 in (81.6 x 100.6 cm), Gift of Alexander Stewart © 1996,
The Art Institute of Chicago; page 7, *Sleeping Baby*, 18 x 24 in (46.3 x 61.9 cm), Courtesy of Sotheby's; page 9, *At the Window*, 25 x 30 in
(62.2 x 75.6 cm), Musée d'Orsay, Paris, Photo R.M.N./Daniel Arnaudet; page 25, *Baby's First Caress*, 24 x 30 in (61 x 76.2 cm), New Britain
Museum of American Art, Connecticut, Harriet Russell Stanley Fund, Photo: E. Irving Blomstrann; page 29, *Mother's Kiss*, 9 x 14 in
(22.9 x 34.9 cm), Worcester Art Museum, Worcester, MA

A Child's Book
of
Lullabies

With paintings by MARY CASSATT
Compiled by SHONA McKELLAR

A Child's Book
of
Lullabies

LULLABIES are more than songs for sleeping. They express the intimate relationship between parent and child in words and music, rhythm and rhyme.

They provide warmth and comfort to a listening youngster.

Long before a child can understand what words mean they will listen to changes of pitch, rhythm, and intonation. As they hear familiar tunes and words repeated they begin to anticipate and recognize the sounds. These are important first steps in the development of speech. Research suggests that children who are sung to early in their lives speak and read slightly earlier than others.

Lullabies help create relaxing and soothing times for both parent and baby. As a child gets older, lullabies can form part of a bedtime routine.

Mary Cassatt's paintings provide in pictures what lullabies provide in words and music. They capture the closeness of the relationship between parent and baby. This is often expressed in physical terms like cuddling and smiling. Cassatt shows us the power of the bond through her expressive artistry.

These are pictures to be shared, especially as babies grow into toddlers. Looking at the lovely, warm pictures, while listening to the lullabies, is a very special experience. The book itself is designed to provide a lasting memory of these early tender moments.

CONTENTS

SLEEP, BABY, SLEEP

Sleep, baby, sleep.
Thy father guards the sheep;
Thy mother shakes the dreamland tree,
Down falls a little dream for thee;
Sleep, baby, sleep.
Sleep, baby, sleep.

Sleep, baby, sleep.
Thy father watches the sheep;
The wind is blowing fierce and wild,
It must not wake my little child;
Sleep, baby, sleep.
Sleep, baby, sleep.

Sleep, baby, sleep.
The large stars are the sheep;
The little stars are the lambs, I guess,
The gentle moon's the shepherdess;
Sleep, baby, sleep.
Sleep, baby, sleep.

Traditional

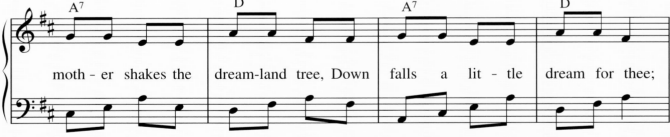

Sleeping Baby, 1880. *Pastel.*

TWINKLE, TWINKLE, LITTLE STAR

Twinkle, twinkle, little star,
How I wonder what you are!
Up above the world so high,
Like a diamond in the sky.
Twinkle, twinkle, little star,
How I wonder what you are!

When the blazing sun is gone,
When he nothing shines upon,
Then you show your little light,
Twinkle, twinkle, all the night.
Twinkle, twinkle, little star,
How I wonder what you are!

Then the traveler in the dark
Thanks you for his tiny spark!
He could not see which way to go
If you did not twinkle so.
Twinkle, twinkle, little star,
How I wonder what you are!

Jane Taylor

Traditional

At the Window, 1889. *Pastel and charcoal on gray paper.*

ROCK-A-BYE, BABY

Rock-a-bye, baby,
On the treetop,
When the wind blows,
The cradle will rock;
When the bough breaks,
The cradle will fall,
Down will come baby,
  cradle and all.

Hush-a-bye, baby,
Up in the sky,
On a soft cloud,
'Tis easy to fly;
When the cloud bursts,
The raindrops will pour,
Down will come baby
  to mother once more.

Traditional

Rock - a - bye, ba — by, On the tree - top,

When the wind blows, The cra - dle will rock;

When the bough breaks, The cra — dle will fall,

Down will come ba - by, cra - dle and all.

The Family, 1892. *Oil on canvas.*

10

HUSH, LITTLE BABY

Hush, little baby, don't say a word,
Papa's gonna buy you a mockingbird;

And if that mockingbird won't sing,
Papa's gonna buy you a diamond ring.

If that diamond ring turns brass,
Papa's gonna buy you a looking glass.

If that looking glass gets broke,
Papa's gonna buy you a billy goat.

If that billy goat won't pull,
Papa's gonna buy you a cart and bull.

If that cart and bull turns over,
Papa's gonna buy you a dog named Rover.

If that dog named Rover won't bark,
Papa's gonna buy you a horse and cart.

If that horse and cart fall down,
You'll still be the sweetest baby in town!

American

Mother and Child, 1890. *Oil on canvas.*

12

NOW THE DAY IS OVER

Now the day is over,
Night is drawing nigh;
Shadows of the evening
Steal across the sky.

Now the darkness gathers,
Stars begin to peep;
Birds and beasts and flowers
Soon will be asleep.

Father, give the weary
Calm and sweet repose;
With thy tender blessing,
May our eyelids close.

Through the long night watches
May thine angels spread
Their white wings above me,
Watching around my bed.

Sabine Baring-Gould

Joseph Barnaby

Mother and Child, 1888. *Pastel.*

BABY'S BOAT

Baby's boat's a silver moon
Sailing in the sky,
Sailing o'er a sea of sleep
While the stars float by.

Chorus
Sail, baby, sail
Out upon that sea;
Only don't forget to sail
Back again to me.

Baby's fishing for a dream,
Fishing far and near.
Her line a silver moonbeam is,
Her bait a silver star.

Chorus
Sail, baby, sail
Out upon that sea;
Only don't forget to sail
Back again to me.

Thomas Decker

The Bath, 1891–92. *Oil on canvas.*

Cum By Yah

Cum by yah, my Lord,
Cum by yah.
Cum by yah, my Lord,
Cum by yah.
Cum by yah, my Lord,
Cum by yah.
Oh Lord, Cum by yah,
Oh Lord, Cum by yah.

Someone's sleepin', Lord,
Cum by yah.
Someone's sleepin', Lord,
Cum by yah.
Someone's sleepin', Lord,
Cum by yah.
Oh Lord, Cum by yah,
Oh Lord, Cum by yah.

Someone's cryin', Lord,
Cum by yah.
Someone's cryin', Lord,
Cum by yah.
Someone's cryin', Lord,
Cum by yah.
Oh Lord, Cum by yah,
Oh Lord, Cum by yah.

Someone's singin', Lord,
Cum by yah . . .

Cum by yah, my Lord,
Cum by yah . . .

African

Sleepy Thomas, Sucking His Thumb, 1893. *Pastel on paper.*

GOLDEN SLUMBERS

Golden slumbers kiss your eyes,
Smiles awake you when you rise.
Sleep, pretty darlings, do not cry,
And I will sing a lullaby:
Rock them, rock them, lullaby.

Care is heavy, therefore sleep you;
You are care and care must keep you.
Sleep, pretty darlings, do not cry,
And I will sing a lullaby:
Rock them, rock them, lullaby.

Thomas Decker

Traditional

Woman and Children, 1906. *Oil on canvas.*

LULLABY AND GOOD NIGHT

Lullaby and good night,
With roses delight,
With lilies bespread
Is baby's wee bed.
Lay thee down now and rest,
May thy slumber be blessed.
Lay thee down now and rest,
May thy slumber be blessed.

Lullaby and good night,
Thy mother's delight,
Bright angels around
My darling shall stand;
They will guard thee from harms,
Thou shalt wake in my arms,
They will guard thee from harms,
Thou shalt wake in my arms.

Fritz Simrock

Brahms

Maternal Kiss, 1896. *Pastel on paper.*

SWEET AND LOW

Sweet and low, sweet and low,
Wind of the western sea;
Low, low, breathe and blow,
Wind of the western sea;
Over the rolling waters go
Come from the dying moon, and blow,
Blow him again to me,
While my little one, while
  my pretty one sleeps.

Sleep and rest, sleep and rest,
Father will come to thee soon;
Rest, rest, on mother's breast,
Father will come to thee soon;
Father will come to his babe in the nest,
Silver sails all out of the west,
Under the silver moon,
Sleep my little one, sleep,
  my pretty one, sleep.

Alfred, Lord Tennyson

Baby's First Caress, 1891. *Pastel on paper.*

CRADLE SONG

Light and rosy be thy slumbers,
Rock'd upon thy mother's breast;
She can lull thee with her numbers,
To the cradled heav'n of rest.

In her heart is love revolving,
Like the planets around the moon.
Hopes and pleasures fondly solving,
Keeping every thought in tune.

Swedish

Mother and Child, 1908. *Oil on canvas.*

26

Go To Sleep

Go to sleep, go to sleep, sleep, sleep.
Go to sleep, little one.
Close your eyes and dream tender dreams,
For you are guarded, protected by my love.

Now go to sleep, go to sleep, sleep, sleep.
Go to sleep, little one.
Close your eyes and dream tender dreams,
For you are guarded, protected by my love.

Long have I waited, I've waited for you.
(Go to sleep.)
Years I spent hoping and praying for you.
(Go to sleep.)
Now that I have you right here by my side,
I will not ever, no, never let you go.

Now go to sleep, go to sleep, sleep, sleep …

Indonesian

Mother's Kiss, 1890–91. *Drypoint and aquatint.*

SLEEP, SLEEP, LITTLE ONE, SLEEP

Sleep, sleep, little one, sleep.
There outside are all the sheep;
Lambs are penned up, safe from harm.
Sleep, my darling, cozy warm.
Sleep, sleep, little one, sleep.

Sleep, sleep, little one, sleep.
Guardian angels watch will keep;
There beneath the apple tree
Gather they sweet dreams for thee.
Sleep, sleep, little one, sleep.

Sleep, sleep, little one, sleep.
See the sky is filled with sheep;
Like a flock the clouds drift by,
Led by moonlit lullaby.
Sleep, sleep, little one, sleep.

French

Mother and Child (no date). *Pastel on paper.*

Self-Portrait, c. 1880. *Watercolor.*

Mary Cassatt – A Biography

Mary Cassatt's work, like that of many Impressionist artists, has a freshness and an appeal to the senses that has ensured popularity for over a century. In her many pictures of mothers and children, Mary Cassatt created timeless images of this most intimate relationship.

1844   Born in Allegheny City, Pennsylvania (now part of Pittsburgh), May 22.
1851   Family moves to Europe, and lives in Paris, France, and Heidelberg and Darmstadt in Germany.
1855   Returns to the United States.
1860   Enrolls as a student at the Pennsylvania Academy of Fine Arts.
1866   Travels to Paris and studies with the painter Charles Chaplin.
1868   First painting is accepted for the Paris Salon.
1870   Returns to Philadelphia due to the outbreak of the Franco-Prussian war.
1871   Visits Italy, copying paintings by Correggio and studying printmaking.
1873   Travels to Spain, Belgium, and Holland to study painting.
1874   First exhibition of the Impressionist painters. The Paris Salon accepts her third painting, which is commented on favorably by Edgar Degas, who is to become a close friend.

1875   Settles permanently in Paris.
1877   Invited to exhibit with the Impressionists. Her parents and sister Lydia come to live in Paris.
1879   Presents eleven works in the fourth Impressionist exhibition. Works with Camille Pissarro and Degas on a journal of original prints.
1880   Participates in the fifth Impressionist exhibition. Arrival of her brother Alexander and his children, who act as models.
1881   Participates in the sixth Impressionist exhibition.
1882   Her sister Lydia dies.
1886   Organizer of, and exhibitor in, the eighth and last Impressionist exhibition. Her paintings are included among Impressionist works shown in New York by the art dealer Paul Durand-Ruel.
1890   Visits exhibition of Japanese prints with Degas in Paris. Begins work on a series of ten color prints.
1891   Her first solo exhibition is shown at Durand-Ruel's gallery. Her father dies.
1892   Receives commission for a mural on the theme of Modern Woman for the World's Fair in Chicago. Purchases Château Beaufresne, at Mesnil-Théribus, in the Oise.
1895   Major individual show at Durand-Ruel's gallery in New York. Her mother dies.
1898   First visit to the United States in twenty years.
1901   Joins her friends the Havemeyers for a trip to Italy and Spain, advising them on acquiring paintings.
1904   Made a *Chevalier de la Légion d'honneur* by the French government.
1906   Her brother Alexander dies.
1908   Makes her last visit to the United States.
1910–11   Visits Egypt with her brother Gardner and his family; Gardner contracts a fatal illness. Cassatt suffers a nervous breakdown.
1914   Awarded the Gold Medal of Honor by the Pennsylvania Academy of Fine Arts. Leaves Beaufresne and retreats to the south of France because of the outbreak of World War I. Stops work due to failing eyesight.
1915   Exhibits with Degas in an exhibition in New York in support of women's suffrage.
1923   Controversy over reprinting of old drypoint plates causes break with Mrs. Havemeyer.
1926   Dies at Beaufresne on June 14.